**W9-BVQ-010**

FREDERICK COUNTY PUBLIC LIBRARIES

A TRUE BOOK™

# The Iroquois

**EMILY J. DOLBEAR
AND PETER BENOIT**

**Children's Press®**
An Imprint of Scholastic Inc.
New York  Toronto  London  Auckland  Sydney
Mexico City  New Delhi  Hong Kong
Danbury, Connecticut

**Content Consultant**
Scott Manning Stevens, PhD
Director, McNickle Center
Newberry Library
Chicago, Illinois

Library of Congress Cataloging-in-Publication Data

Dolbear, Emily J.
  The Iroquois/Emily J. Dolbear and Peter Benoit.
      p. cm.—(A true book)
  Includes bibliographical references and index.
  ISBN-13: 978-0-531-20771-0 (lib. bdg.)          978-0-531-29313-3 (pbk.)
  ISBN-10: 0-531-20771-4 (lib. bdg.)              0-531-29313-0 (pbk.)
1. Iroquois Indians—Juvenile literature. I. Benoit, Peter, 1955– II. Title.
  E99.I7D59 2011
  974.7004'9755—dc22                              2010049079

No part of this publication may be reproduced in whole or in part, or stored in a retrieval system, or transmitted in any form or by any means, electronic, mechanical, photocopying, recording, or otherwise, without written permission of the publisher. For information regarding permission, write to Scholastic Inc., Attention: Permissions Department, 557 Broadway, New York, NY 10012.

© 2011 Scholastic Inc.

All rights reserved. Published in 2011 by Children's Press, an imprint of Scholastic Inc.
Printed in China 62
SCHOLASTIC, CHILDREN'S PRESS, A TRUE BOOK and associated logos are trademarks and/or registered trademarks of Scholastic Inc.

2 3 4 5 6 7 8 9 10 R 19 18 17 16 15 14 13 12

# Find the Truth!

**Everything** you are about to read is true *except* for one of the sentences on this page.

Which one is **TRUE**?

**T or F**  Clan mothers played an important role within the Iroquois community.

**T or F**  The Iroquois refer to themselves as "Iroquois."

Find the answers in this book.

Iroquois corn husk doll

# Contents

## THE **BIG** TRUTH!

### Baggataway

**Iroquois
lacrosse player**

4

Iroquois pottery

Iroquois longhouses lasted roughly 20 years before beginning to rot.

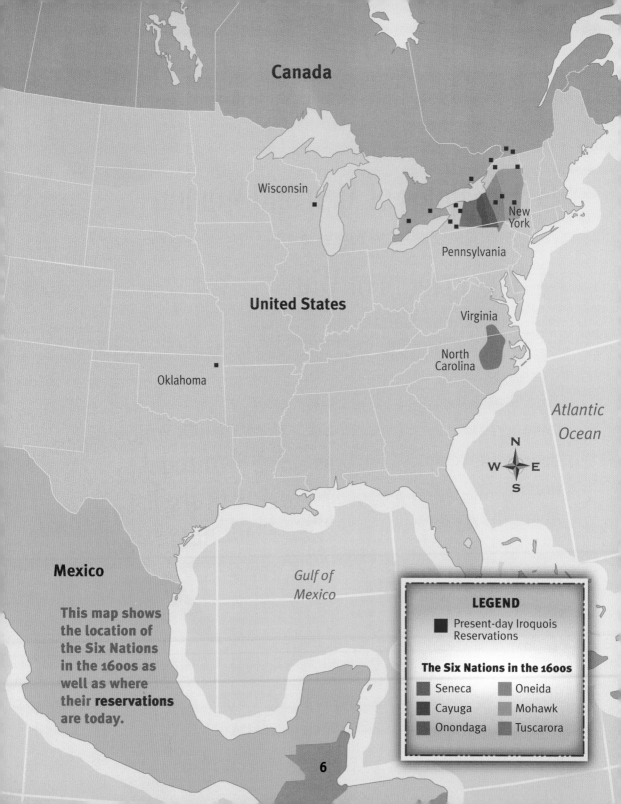

Canada

Wisconsin

New York

Pennsylvania

United States

Virginia

North Carolina

Oklahoma

Atlantic Ocean

N
W · E
S

Mexico

Gulf of Mexico

This map shows the location of the Six Nations in the 1600s as well as where their **reservations** are today.

**LEGEND**

Present-day Iroquois Reservations

**The Six Nations in the 1600s**

Seneca          Oneida

Cayuga          Mohawk

Onondaga        Tuscarora

6

# CHAPTER 1

# A League of Nations

The Iroquois (IHR-uh-kwoy) are a Native American people with a long, fascinating history. Early Iroquois lived in today's New York State more than 2,000 years ago.

The Iroquois were not a single tribe. They came from five tribes, or nations: the Seneca, Cayuga (ky-UH-gah), Onondaga (oh-non-DA-gah), Oneida (oh-NYE-dah), and Mohawk. The tribes spoke different **dialects** of the Iroquois language. Sometimes, they fought each other. They also fought the Algonquin and Huron tribes.

The Peacemaker stands among Iroquois leaders of the Five Nations.

# The Five Nations

According to Iroquois tradition, a leader called the Peacemaker worked to end fighting among the Iroquois tribes. With help from an Onondaga man named Ayenwatha (ah-yon-WAT-ha), the Peacemaker advised the chiefs of the five tribes to make peace. Instead of each tribe working separately, one Iroquois **League**—the Five Nations—could reach common goals by working together. Most chiefs agreed with this plan, but the Onondaga chief Tadodaho (tuh-doe-DAH-ho) took longer to convince.

# Tadodaho, Chief of the Onondaga Nation

Iroquois stories say that Chief Tadodaho had snakes in his hair and a twisted body. People believed he could kill enemies at a distance, without even seeing them. The Peacemaker held a ceremony to soothe Tadodaho, straighten his matted hair, and remove the twists from his body. At last, Tadodaho agreed to the Iroquois Great Law of Peace. That is the story of how the Onondaga people joined the Iroquois League.

# The Great Law of Peace

The Great Law of Peace outlined the basic rules and laws for governing the Iroquois League. It was a kind of **constitution**. The Great Law of Peace was, at first, a spoken agreement. Its 117 parts, or articles, were recorded and passed on by weaving together patterns of tube-shaped beads called **wampum**. The beads were woven to create symbols and shapes that stood for different ideas or words. The Iroquois read the information aloud when it was needed at meetings. The articles were written down many years later.

These men carry wampum belts recording major agreements between the Iroquois and settlers or colonizers.

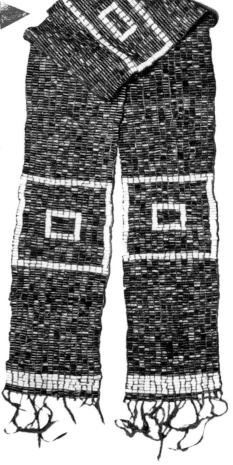

White beads symbolized peace.

**Iroquois wampum belt**

# Wampum

Wampum, made of white and purple Atlantic coast seashells, was an important Iroquois tradition. Women rounded and smoothed small pieces of shells into individual wampum beads and pierced them to string together. Tribal members attached the wampum to deer hide and created elaborate belts. Chiefs carried these belts during tribal ceremonies. The bead patterns also recorded important events and agreements such as the Great Law of Peace.

# The Arrival of Europeans

European explorers and traders began arriving in mainland North America in the 1500s. They came from different countries, including England, Spain, France, and the Netherlands. The Iroquois League formed about this time.

Jacques Cartier was a French explorer who traveled to North America in search of a shorter route to Asia. He met Iroquois and other native groups on his voyages.

An Iroquois group showed Cartier how to make a tea rich in vitamin C.

Native Americans traded furs with the Dutch in exchange for kettles and other goods.

# Trading and Warring

The Iroquois began trading beaver **pelts** with
the Dutch and the English. Supported by their
new trading partners, the Iroquois extended their
territory further into the Great Lakes region. There
they defeated Algonquin tribes, who were backed
by the French. These Iroquois victories gave the
tribe a larger share of land and the beaver fur trade.

**The French and Iroquois in conflict. As the French began to fear British expansion, they befriended the Iroquois. The treaty they signed in 1701 was called the Great Peace of Montreal.**

# Peace With the French

During the first half of the 1600s, the Iroquois were at the height of their power. They were known as far south as today's Virginia. But they began to suffer when the number of French in Canada grew, which helped the Algonquin become stronger. In 1701, the Iroquois agreed to a peace **treaty** with the French.

## A Sixth Nation

In the first few decades of the 18th century, the British settled what is today's North Carolina. The Native Americans there—the Tuscarora (tuss-kuh-ROHR-uh) Indians—fled north. The Tuscarora Indians joined the Iroquois League as the sixth nation in 1722. Though they had been located far from the other nations in the league, the Tuscarora already spoke an Iroquoian language. They were the final Indian group to join the Iroquois League.

Some Tuscarora were sold as slaves by English traders.

Constant conflict, which grew into war with the British settlers, eventually drove the Tuscarora north.

These recreations show what Iroquois dwellings looked like. Many Iroquois villages contained more than 100 longhouses.

# CHAPTER 2

# People of the Longhouse

When the Iroquois League was first formed, the Peacemaker named the Five Nations Haudenosaunee (HO-den-oh-SHO-nee). It means "people of the **longhouse**." Members of the tribe still call themselves Haudenosaunee. It was the French settlers who called them Iroquois.

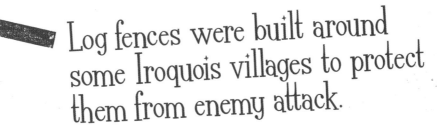

Log fences were built around some Iroquois villages to protect them from enemy attack.

17

# Clans in Longhouses

The name "people of the longhouse" explains where and how the Iroquois lived. Iroquois families lived in long buildings, or longhouses. A longhouse was home to a large family group called a **clan**. Most of the family was related through the mother's clan. Marriages could not take place between two members of the same clan.

**Sometimes, 15 to 20 families lived in a longhouse.**

Some longhouses were longer than football fields.

# Longhouse Sizes

Longhouses came in many sizes. A traditional longhouse was about 200 feet (60 meters) long and 18 feet (5 m) wide. The top peak of the sloping roof stood 18 feet (5 m) high.

Longhouses had fireplaces to keep them warm. Holes along the roof allowed smoke to escape.

**Everything had its place in a longhouse. Shelves were used for storage, and some foods were hung from the ceiling to dry.**

# Building Longhouses

To build a longhouse, workers set wooden poles in the ground. They used cross poles running the length of the building to brace the walls. Then they bent a series of poles to make the roof. The framework was covered with bark and sewn in place. The longhouse had doors at both ends.

**Men and women helped build different parts of a longhouse.**

The Peacemaker urged the Iroquois to think of the League as a kind of longhouse.

The Mohawk were the first to join the Iroquois League.

## One Family

The Peacemaker wanted the tribes to think of themselves as one family. He wanted people to think of the Iroquois League as a longhouse. For example, the Seneca, as the most westerly tribe, were called Keepers of the Western Door. The Mohawk were the Keepers of the Eastern Door. The Onondaga, in the middle, were Keepers of the Central Flame. The Onondaga tended a ceremonial fire for the Iroquois League.

# The Grand Council

The Peacemaker also determined in the Great Law of Peace that the Iroquois Nations should have a **council**. This council, called the Grand Council, was made up of 50 chiefs, or **sachems**. The sachems were chosen to make decisions for the league. They openly discussed and generally agreed on final decisions.

The Peacemaker is said to have compared the Five Nations to five arrows. A single arrow could easily be broken, but five bound together could not.

The Iroquois village of Onandaga Hollow was located near present-day Syracuse, New York.

# The Onondaga Nation

Central to the Grand Council was the Onondaga Nation. It had 14 sachems. The Cayuga people had only 10, the Oneida and Mohawk Nations had 9 sachems each, and the Seneca people had 8. As the last joining nation, the Tuscarora Indians had no official council members.

The Grand Council's spiritual leader was always an Onondaga man, a tradition that continues to this day. Even today, he is called the Tadodaho, in honor of the chief whose consent made the Iroquois League possible.

# Baggataway

Many Native American groups played stick and ball games. The Iroquois were playing a game called baggataway for centuries before the Europeans came. In 1636, a French missionary saw the game being played. Sticks with baskets on one end were used to pass the ball back and forth as the teams tried to score goals on each other. He described it as "the game of la crosse," because the shape of the sticks reminded him of a bishop's staff, or "la crosse." The name stuck, and the game has spread around the world.

The playing field was sometimes miles long, with hundreds of players on either team. A single game might last for days.

The Iroquois believed that the game was a gift from the Creator. It encourages health and strength, and brings the nations together. It was played for entertainment, but also as a ritual.

Today, the Federation of International Lacrosse holds a world championship every four years. Nations around the world—including the Iroquois Nation—are members.

Iroquois women and men had clearly defined responsibilities. But neither men nor women were more important in Iroquois society.

# CHAPTER 3

# The Roles of Men and Women

Women had a lot of power in Iroquois society. Their influence came from the basic beliefs of the Haudenosaunee. The Haudenosaunee believed in twin spirit beings named Sapling and Flint. They were two halves of a greater whole, representing divine will and its opposite force. Each half was thought to balance the other. The same was thought of men and women in Iroquois society.

Births of baby girls were celebrated because they would eventually become mothers and add members to the clan.

# Field and Forest

Iroquois women did all the work involving the fields. They farmed, gathered food, and kept the home in order. Some items women gathered were wild roots, berries, nuts, and herbs for medicine. Men did all work that related to the forest. They hunted, traded, and fought. Men hunted for deer and wild turkey, and fished for salmon, bass, and trout.

**The Iroquois attached spears or hooks to the ends of lines to catch fish.**

# The Three Sisters

corn plant

The Iroquois people farmed from early in their history and depended on crops to survive. They grew maize (corn), beans, and squash together so each plant helped the other two grow better. The Iroquois people called these crops the Three Sisters and considered them the Creator's special gift.

**Growing the Three Sisters together is smart. Cornstalks support the climbing bean vines. Beans give nutrients to the soil. Squash leaves shade the soil, keeping it moist.**

bean plant

squash plant

**Cooperating and dividing chores helped the Iroquois get the day's work done.**

# Shared Work

The tribe gave land to different clans to farm. People often shared ownership of the land. Women went from field to field, working together in large groups. The men also hunted in groups. They might join together to build a large brush fence to capture whole herds of deer at once. They shared game and fish with the entire village.

# A Child's Life

The Iroquois people always worked for the good of their clan. Children were taught to be strong and to think for themselves. They had their own daily tasks at home and in the fields to help them learn the ways of their elders. A mother and her family were responsible for the children.

Children played in the fields. By making noise, they scared crop-eating animals.

Iroquois children helped their mothers plant crops and do other work in the fields.

31

Women controlled agriculture and food distribution within the clan.

## The Mother's Clan and Longhouse

An Iroquois man lived in the longhouse of his wife's clan. If he did not work hard, his wife could ask him to leave. Children always remained with their mother, attached to her clan, and lived in the longhouse of her people. An Iroquois woman could own land, horses, and housing. Her property before marriage remained hers. It did not pass to the man after marriage.

# Clan Mothers

Women had power in the clan and in the league as a whole. Iroquois female leaders in the clans were called clan mothers. A group called the Clan Mothers' Council decided how to hand out land. If a clan did not take good care of its land, the clan mothers could give it to someone else. This council could even remove the chief of a clan. The oldest woman in the chief's family was responsible for naming the person who would replace the chief.

Clan mothers, such as Audrey Shenendoah of the Onandoga, are still active in the Iroquois today.

# Power in the League

All 50 sachems in the Grand Council were men. However, clan mothers chose the sachems. If a sachem could not reach an agreement with the women of his tribe, or if he ignored the Great Law of Peace, a clan mother could remove him from the council. She did this by removing the deer horns from his headgear. It was called "knocking off the horns."

**A council of Mohawk women speaks to a group of sachems.**

34

Some experts believe that certain ideas in the U.S. Constitution came, in part, from the Iroquois League's system of government.

## An Equal Share

No Iroquois treaty was official until three-fourths of male voters and an equal share of clan mothers approved it. The power and independence that the Iroquois system gave its women was unusual for the time.

After the Revolutionary War, Thayendanegea (Joseph Brant) and his Mohawk chiefs were given land near Grand River, Ontario, Canada.

# CHAPTER 4

# The Effects of War

Over the years, the Iroquois League lost many members warring with other tribes and Europeans. The Iroquois sometimes led attacks to take prisoners, usually children or young men. They then raised the prisoners in the ways of the Iroquois. This is how the Iroquois could replace men lost in warfare. In time, the Iroquois League came to include people from the Huron and Algonquin tribes, among others.

 Many native groups did not fight at night. The Iroquois believed the sun enjoyed seeing their bravery.

# Trading for Weapons

The Iroquois began using European steel weapons, instead of bows and arrows, in their battles. The Iroquois traded beaver pelts for things they could not produce, such as rifles and metal axes. The Iroquois gradually depended on trade, especially with the British, for gunpowder, too. In this way, the British won Iroquois support for their wars against the French in the 1700s.

**An official representing Britain meets with the Mohawk. Such officials worked to persuade the Iroquois to defend British interests.**

American forces battle the British and their Mohawk supporters during the American Revolutionary War. Many Iroquois lost their lives in the war.

Some Iroquois referred to the colonies as "the 13 fires."

# Choosing Sides

The American **Revolutionary War**, which gave the 13 American colonies independence from Great Britain, began in 1775. The Iroquois League allowed each nation to choose a side in the conflict. Most of the Iroquois chose to fight alongside the British. They believed helping the British win would guarantee Iroquois control of Iroquois land. The Oneida and some of the Tuscarora people sided with the Americans.

# Iroquois in the War

Mohawk Indian chief Joseph Brant helped persuade four of the six Iroquois nations to remain allies of Britain. After the British lost, Brant helped secure land from Britain for his people in Ontario, Canada. Chief Cornplanter and his Seneca warriors also fought alongside the British in the Revolutionary War.

# An Iroquois Timeline

## Between 1400 and 1600

**Five tribes—the Mohawk, Oneida, Onondaga, Cayuga, and Seneca— form the Iroquois League in the Northeast.**

**1722**

**A sixth nation, the Tuscarora tribe, joins the Iroquois League.**

# A Loss of Land

After the war ended in 1783, the Iroquois League lost most of its land to the new country of the United States of America. Its people were forced to settle on small reservations. Today, many of them live on Iroquois land in New York, Wisconsin, and Oklahoma, and Canada's Ontario and Quebec.

## 21st century

There are about 80,000 Iroquois in North America.

## 1754 to 1763 ➡

The Iroquois League fights alongside the British to defeat the French in North America.

## 1775-1783

The Iroquois—except for the Oneida and some Tuscarora, who sided with the Americans—fight as allies of the British in the Revolutionary War.

# The Haudenosaunee

The Great Peacemaker brought together five, and then six, Iroquois nations. These nations put into practice the Great Law of Peace with its councils. They survived European warring and disease. They considered the longhouse a symbol of the Iroquois League. The Iroquois tribes may no longer live in bark-covered homes, but they will always be the Haudenosaunee—the people of the longhouse. ★

**A woman speaks about growing up as a member of the Onondaga Nation during an event aimed at improving the relationship between the Iroquois and the United States.**

# True Statistics

**Number of Iroquois Indians today:** 80,000

**Number of members on the Grand Council of the Iroquois League:** 50

**Number of articles in the Great Law of Peace:** 117

**Length of some Iroquois longhouses:** 200 ft. (60 m)

**Number of tribes in the Iroquois League before 1722:** 5

**Number of tribes in the Iroquois League after 1722:** 6

The Iroquois used rattles such as this one as part of their ceremonial dances.

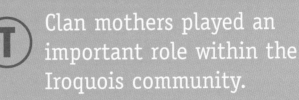

## Did you find the truth?

**(T)** Clan mothers played an important role within the Iroquois community.

**(F)** The Iroquois referred to themselves as "Iroquois."

# Resources

## Books

Bial, Raymond. *Longhouses*. New York: Children's Press, 2004.

Shenandoah, Joanne, and Douglas M. George. *Skywoman: Legends of the Iroquois*. Santa Fe, NM: Clear Light Publishers, 1996.

St. Lawrence, Genevieve. *The Iroquois and Their History*. Minneapolis: Compass Point Books, 2006.

Wilcox, Charlotte. *The Iroquois*. Minneapolis: Lerner Publications, 2007.

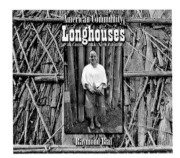

# Organizations and Web Sites

## Constitution of the Iroquois Nations
www.constitution.org/cons/iroquois.htm
Read the text of the constitution of the Iroquois League.

## Seneca Nation of Indians
www.sni.org
Learn more about present and past Seneca culture.

## St. Regis Mohawk Tribe
www.srmt-nsn.gov
Learn about present and past Mohawk culture.

# Places to Visit

## Ganondagan State Historic Site
1488 State Route 444
Victor, NY 14564
(585) 924-5848
www.ganondagan.org
Take a trip to this 17th-century Seneca town, complete with a traditional longhouse.

## Iroquois Indian Museum
324 Caverns Road, P.O. Box 7
Howes Cave, NY 12092
(518) 296-8949
www.iroquoismuseum.org
Visit this educational institution dedicated to the Iroquois culture.

# Important Words

**clan** (KLAN) —a large family group

**constitution** (kon-stuh-TOO-shuhn) —basic laws and rules for government

**council** (KOUN-suhl) —a group of people chosen to make decisions

**dialects** (DYE-uh-lektss) —different forms of a single language

**league** (LEEG) —a group of people, teams, states, or nations

**longhouse** (LAWNG-houss) —a long building where Iroquois clans live

**pelts** (PELTZ) —furry animal skins

**reservations** (rez-ur-VAY-shuhnz) —areas of land set aside for Native Americans to live on

**Revolutionary War** (rev-uh-LOO-shuhn-air-ee WOR) —a war from 1775 to 1783 that gave the 13 American colonies independence from Great Britain, forming the United States of America

**sachems** (SAY-chumz) —members of the Great Council of the Iroquois League; powerful chiefs

**treaty** (TREE-tee) —a formal peace or trade agreement

**wampum** (WAHM-puhm) —tube-shaped beads made from polished shells and used in trade or ceremonies

# Index

Page numbers in **bold** indicate illustrations

47

# About the Authors

Emily J. Dolbear works as a freelance editor and writer of children's books. She lives with her family in Brookline, Massachusetts.

Peter Benoit is educated as a mathematician but has many other interests. He has taught and tutored high school and college students for many years, mostly in math and science. He also runs summer workshops for writers and students of literature. Benoit has written more than 2,000 poems. His life has been one committed to learning. He lives in Greenwich, New York.

**PHOTOGRAPHS** © 2011: Alamy Images: 5 bottom, 15, 18, 41 left (North Wind Picture Archives), 20 (Stock Montage, Inc.); AP Images: 33 (Heather Ainsworth), cover (Mike Okoniewski/New York State Fair); Clifford Oliver Photography/www.cliffordoliverphotography.com: 48 bottom; Corbis Images: 30 (Bettmann), 4, 25 center, 25 right (Ramin Talaie), 16 (Marilyn Angel Wynn/Nativestock.com); Getty Images: back cover, 41 right (Marilyn Angel Wynn/Nativestock.com); Landov, LLC: 19 (Chromorange/dpa); Mary E. Dolbear: 48 top; Matthew Parker/Painting by Lazare & Parker: 32; National Geographic Stock/Jack Unruh: 31; Nativestock. com/Marilyn "Angel" Wynn: 22, 29; Photo Researchers, NY/Aaron Haupt: 35; Photolibrary: 3, 43 (Marilyn Angel Wynn/Nativestock.com); Raymond Bial: 21; Scholastic Library Publishing, Inc.: 44; The Art Archive/ Picture Desk: 24, 25 left, 25 background (George Catlin/Buffalo Bill Historical Center, Cody, WY/Gift of Mrs. Sidney T. Miller); The Design Lab: 6; The Granger Collection, New York: 28 (Felix O.C. Darley), 38 (Henry Dawkins), 12, 14, 36 (C.W. Jefferys), 8, 11, 13, 23, 26, 34, 39; The Image Works: 5 top, 40 (Werner Forman/ Topham), 10 (Mike Greenlar), 42 (L. Long/Syracuse Newspapers), 9 (SSPL).

MAR 2014

2 1982 03014 5290